THE MOUTH OF GOLD.

A SERIES OF

DRAMATIC SKETCHES

ILLUSTRATING THE LIFE AND TIMES OF

CHRYSOSTOM.

BY EDWIN JOHNSON.

A. S. BARNES & CO.
NEW YORK AND CHICAGO:
1873.

INTRODUCTORY NOTE.

THE materials for these sketches have been derived mainly from the biographies of CHRYSOSTOM by Neander and Perthes. I have, in some instances, followed closely the translation of the latter work by Hovey and Ford.

It was not till the following pages had been stereotyped that I learned of another biography, recently issued in England by Rev. W. R. W. Stephens, M. A. Its perusal might, here and there, have given a different color to the representation I have made; if indeed I might not have deemed a version in the present form superfluous, in view of the elaborate and highly interesting treatment of the theme by the new volume. I trust, however, that I have not seriously erred from historical accuracy, and that books so essentially different in plan may be mutually helpful in diffusing a knowledge of one who well deserves to be known and honored always and everywhere.

My aim being to present a condensed and, at the same time, vivid picture of the man and of the scenes and characters that surrounded him, the dramatic form seemed to me suitable. But my little book aspires not to the dignity of a drama. It is only as the title page indicates: *a series of dramatic sketches.*

E. J.

MAY, 1873.

TO

S. K. J

I.

PERSONS REPRESENTED.

JOHN, *surnamed* CHRYSOSTOM.
PAULUS, *a young man of Antioch.*
FLAVIAN, " " " *Rome.*
GLAUCUS, " " " *Antioch.*
ACHMED, *an Arabian trader.*
ANTHUSA, *mother of* JOHN.

SCENE.—*Antioch, in Syria.*
TIME.—A. D. 370.

SCENE I.—*The Arcade.*

Enter PAULUS *and* FLAVIAN.

Paul. Is it not fair?
Fla. More fair than you had told,
Or I had dreamed. The Greeks are only just
When from the brows of candidates at home—
Athens and Corinth—they withhold the crown,
Assigning it to this bright Syrian city,
As Paris gave the golden fruit to Venus.
Fit appellation joins the name when men
Do speak of ANTIOCH *the beautiful.*
Paul. See where her statue stands, a radiant queen
Whose feet rest on the rising river-god
Orontes. Lofty Libanus looks down,
With fostering love, upon the city's face,
Like a fond mother on the child she folds;
And Taurus, towering opposite, defies
The harsh North-wind to march his forces hither.
Fla. A better safeguard than the circling hills
Hath set its sign upon yon crag you call
Mount Silphius, where the royal bird alighting

Informed Seleucus here to found his city.
Now crowns the height, as if from Rome transferred
A temple consecrate to Jupiter,
Whose power propitious can alone defend
Cities and men.

Paul. And yet we lack assurance
The king of gods can curb the Vulcan crew
That underneath this soil are wont to work,
Till the tremendous blasting splits their roof—
Which is our floor—and we, poor souls, are put
In fear and peril of an utter fall.
If piety can save, we are most safe:
For not alone to Jupiter we pray,
And to the host who hail him as their head;
From Palestine are come the worshippers
Of Him they name Jehovah, Israel's God;
A hundred thousand wear the title fixed
At Antioch first upon a feeble band
Who followed Christ: the title blazoned since
Upon imperial standards, and embraced
By multitudes throughout the realm.

Fla. Tell me
The manner of your Christian folk.

Paul. Why much
The manner of us all: for Antioch
Assimilates all strange diversity.

As in the swift Orontes meet and merge
The waters trickling forth from far-off founts
Among the frozen hills, and those that leave,
Reluctantly, the flowery meads, and those
That plunge impetuous from the nearer heights,
So doth our social current sweep all sects
And sorts along in frolic motion. See!
The stream is swelling now, as with a freshet.
The voice of Daphne calls her votaries;
And through this arched and shady way they pour—
The Greek and Arab, Persian, Jew and Gaul—
Costumes and dialects diverse, but minds
Intent alike on pleasure.

Fla. Windingly,
Nor without stain of sordid contact runs
Orontes: if report be true, the tide
Of pleasure here runs at its wayward will,
And not too limpid! [*Enter* GLAUCUS.

Paul. Here's a Christian friend.—
Ho, Glaucus, whither bound? and wherefore hold
Your course so breezily that lazy barques,
As this good friend from Rome and I myself,
Are like to be run down by you and sunk
Incontinently?

Glau. Pardon, Flavian;
Your pardon, both; and for my punishment

I'll let the charms that drew me, as with chains,
Float out of sight. Fortune may send betimes
This way some other fair for company.
Oh what were Daphne's fountains, groves and flowers
Without the light of love revealing them?
Paul. Enough of that. But tell us of the race
Wherein your faction yesterday took part.

> "Sunt quos curriculo pulverem Olympicum
> Collegisse juvat metaque fervidis
> Evitata rotis palmaque nobilis—"

Glau. And you not there?
Paul. Nay; for the envious wind,
Though fervently invoked to waft us up
From port Seleucia, where I met my friend,
Fell off, and left us, fretting at our fate,
To lie inert, while you and all the town
Enjoyed your holiday.
Glau. Rare holiday!
The sun bade every vapor that could break
His view withdraw, and with wide-open eye
Gazed down upon the concave field that swarmed
With scholars, soldiers, citizens and priests,
Plebeians and patricians, beauty, youth
And honor. First the wrestlers played their part;
And then the rival ranks of green and blue,
Ranged opposite each other, watched the course.

Fla. You wear the green.
Glau. And proud am I to wear it.—
Four chariots, burnished bright as Phœbus' own,
Flashed suddenly upon the field. Their steeds—
The best of rich Arabia's race—ill brooked
Restraint till all was ready. Ardent rays
Shot from their eyes and nostrils. On their backs
The gilded harnesses sat quivering.
Each lithe and keen-eyed charioteer braced firm
His feet, and tugged the reins.
A bugle note!
And, as an arrow leaves the twanging cord,
Those eager steeds sprang forward. Then uprose
A shout from all the multitude; but soon
Suspense kept silence, while, obscured in dust,
The champions sped from sight. The cloud of dust
Recedes and falls. But now another cloud
Arises. Scarcely seen at first, it grows
Substantial, growing nearer, moving on
Amidst a mingled murmur of applause
And rage. A chariot overturned! A horse
Dragging his driver by the tangled reins
Lifeless, himself a mass of foam and blood!
I marked, amidst the flying ruin, well
A badge of blue, and then I lent my voice
To swell the volumed note of victory.

Fla. The charioteer was dead?
Glau. Never again
His skill shall threaten our defeat. The wreck
Was scarce removed when, following a sound
Like rumbling thunder, rushed four steeds in sight.
They rather flew than ran. The foremost pair
Were decked with green; and at each moment made
A wider space behind their whirling wheels.
I wonder if our uproar reached you not
When, seizing Lucius from his glowing car,
We bore him on our shoulders to and fro;
We soothed and crowned the panting steeds, and danced,
And drained such bumpers as the god of wine
Himself might pour.
The vanquished soon forsook
The field. And prudently: for some light word
Of scorn, let fall by them or us, had struck
Perchance the signal of a bloody strife.
But why recall the taste of pleasures past?
To-day holds to our lips a cup brimful
Of joyance. Come with me to Daphne's bowers.
Paul. Our feet shall follow yours more leisurely.
Glau. Then, for the present, *Fare ye well.*
Paul and Fla. Farewell. [*Exit Glaucus.*
Fla. If all the sect are weighted light as he,

'Tis hardly strange it has outstripped so soon
Religions older than itself.

Paul. Haply
The next whom we encounter may be one
Whom other than Olympic strifes inflame—
An athlete on the philosophic field,
Delighting in the dust of disputation.
The web of gossamer is not so fine
As are the threads these subtle thinkers spin ;
And in the metaphysic mesh they lie,
Intent to catch and bind, with syllogism
And curious lore, the unwary and unskilled.
Or forth they sally, armed with wits more keen
Than are the blades Damascus fabricates.
Amidst the clash of words with words, we hear,
Confusedly, of Father and of Son,
Of substance and of essence infinite,
Of pre-existence and fatality,
Of angel natures and accomplishments,
And oh, I know not what of themes too high
Or quiddities too fine for mortal sight,
But all the more provocative of zeal,
As lightest tinder kindles quickest fire.

Fla. And have you none of those fanatic men
Who fly from life to dull monastic cells ;
Or who from caves and grottoes grim dislodge

The savage animals and reptile tribes,
To make themselves a tomb-like dwelling-place?

Paul. Oh, yes; yon hillsides swarm with holy monks.

Fla. I see approaching us an old acquaintance.

[*Enter* ACHMED.

What brings thee hither, Achmed, from thy home
In far Arabia?

Ach. Faith, a camel brought me.
Upon his ridgy back I rocked across
The desert, under skies of fire, to find
In Antioch, a Roman whom I met
Long since in Alexandria. Wherefore here?

Fla. For pleasure, not for pelf. I'll warrant *thou*
Art occupied with thoughts of gain. Tell us—
We are no thieves—what hast thou in thy pack?

Ach. Stand close, and you shall hear.

Beyond that height
Which hides a curve in the Orontes, lies
A little camp. Ten camels crouch beneath
The sycamores that throw a friendly shade.
Arbutus, myrtle, bay and fig-tree grace
The shore that seems thrice beautiful to eyes
Accustomed to the sandy wastes. My men
Keep watch, while I within the city search

For some rich dealer who may buy with gold
My store of myrrh and aloes, grain and gum.
Paul. I know the man—a Jew, whose pile of coin
Would scarce a diminution own, although
For all thy goods he gave thee twice their worth.
We'll go together to his dismal house.
Ach. Why then I'll show you presently some strings
Of pearls, more pure and large than ever yet
The brows or necks of empresses have worn.
I wish—in answer to your courtesy—
Your lady-loves might be festooned with them.

SCENE II.—*A Room in Anthusa's house.*

Enter ANTHUSA *and* JOHN.

John. Urge me not, mother, to abide with thee,
But, with thy blessing, bid me seek the cloister.
Anth. Bethink thee how the Moabitess Ruth
Addressed to Naomi, who was her mother
By marriage only, words unlike to thine.
'Entreat me not to leave thee'—was her cry;

But thine, 'Entreat me not stay with thee.'
Oh dire fatality of modern days!
The pulse of filial love no longer beats.
John. Not lack of filial love forbids my stay;
But loyalty to One whose claim I hold
Superior to every human tie.
Anth. Yet Mary's son, whom death alone removed
From her whose soul was pierced with pain, left not
The widow childless. Mortal agony
Could not divide his thoughts from her. I see
To-day his look of tender pity fall
Upon another woman, and I hear
His voice address a well-beloved John:
'Behold thy mother!'
While my bridal robe
Was bright, Death folded it away forever.
The meek and matron robe was mine ere yet
The years of youth were fled; but when he fell
On whom I leaned so lovingly, I clung
More close to one who wore his image dear.
'This little one,' I said, 'will be a man
When life with me has passed meridian.
As bees lay by in store for days of dearth,
I'll treasure up in him all precious things
Of strength, of knowledge and of piety:

So, in my weak and wintry season, want
Shall touch me not.' Alas! thou wouldst defraud
And leave me twice a widow. Wait, I pray,
Till my removal hence shall break thy bonds.
John. My mother, this is not like thee. My boast
Has been that thou wert strong and full of faith,
Afraid of nothing but of sin. Full well
I know the story of thy life—a life
Made up of sacrifice for God and me.
Though princely suitors came, they kneeled in vain
To win a heart pre-occupied. Thy home—
An isle of peace amidst a sea of sin—
Was kept for me, and here my mind was moulded.
As Moses trod the halls of palaces
And learned the lore of Egypt's heathen schools,
Yet kept the love of country and of God
A mother's lips and life had breathed upon him,
So fell away from me the arguments
Of Pagan teachers and the charms of vice,
Because I felt my mother's nobleness
And purity. Libanius himself,
My tutor, filled with scorn of Christian truth
And fired with proselyting zeal, exclaimed,
Before the miracle of character
Like thine, 'What mothers do these Christians have!'

Anth. Thy praise is sweet, but sweeter is thy presence.

John. Should I unlearn the lesson thou hast taught,
And turn my back upon the chosen goal?
Ambition marked for me a shining track:
By learning and by eloquence to win
The meed of praise and rich emolument
Within the forum. Soon I found what arts
And fallacies and modes unclean pollute
The fane of justice, taint the name of law,
And make the advocate himself too oft
The criminal. In sorrow and disgust
I turned away, resolved henceforth to be
CHRIST'S advocate. The purpose thou didst bless.

Anth. But wherefore seek in cloistered solitude
To serve the Master who himself was found
In synagogues and in the market-place,
An open publisher of truth?

John. To quench
The fires of sensual passion in ourselves—
To scourge our pride and appetite—to prune
The branches, that the fruit may thrive—is not
The better part of service this? But thou,
My mother, little can thy pure heart know
How stern the task imposed on grosser nature,
When it would conquer earthliness and rise

Superior to self. I would have leave
To fight upon a vantage ground.
Anth. I doubt
The advantage, oh my son; for so it seems
To my poor thought as if a nation pent
Within itself should breed intestine strife
And feverish anarchy; whereas if set
Confronting foreign arms, the factions all
Would league, to subjugate the common foe.
Disease but seldom dares to strike the man
Who comes to conquer it: more oft it seeks
The fugitive who yields to craven fear.
To govern, not exterminate the powers
Our Father gave, I deem the soul's high province.
The cross indeed is ours, but needing not
That we should seek for it nor fashion it:
In daily duties will its form appear.
John. I know not if the life monastic be
A cross in such a time, when riot reigns
With revelry, the State is stirred with strife,
The church itself is filled with worldliness,
With love of power and love of pleasures vain.
Well might we covet, as the Psalmist did,
'Wings like the dove that we might fly to rest.'
Anth. Beware, or selfishness will steal and claim
The guise of virtue. Christ came down from rest
And residence celestial, here to toil

And die, that he might better a bad world.
He bids us follow him; but sends a Dove
To brood with wings of comfort o'er our hearts
And bear us oft in spirit home to rest.
Enough, till he shall call us hence forever.

John. I yield: and yet if in retiracy
And prayer and study of God's Book, the years
Might pass till I should hear the call divine
As Paul, the Apostle, heard it when he left
Arabian solitudes to preach the Christ,
So might I hope to be the minister
Of greater good to men.

Anth. I thank thee, Lord!—
Hadst thou, my son, from this thy youthful home
Gone forth to make a new one and a dearer,
My fondest earthly wish had been fulfilled.
'Tis well: I question neither God nor thee.
Do thou His will. But oh, 'tis not His will
That I should lack the solace of thy face
And daily speech, till human love is lost
In love divine. Then, filial duty done,
Thou shalt be free, and God will show thy way
And crown thy life with good.

John. Of such a mother,
The Lord help me to be a worthy son;
And late receive her to His Paradise!

II.

PERSONS REPRESENTED.

Chrysostom, Paulus, Glaucus.
Cæsarius *and* Hellebichus, *Judges.*
Macedonius, *a Monk.*
Soothsayer, Officers, Rioters.

SCENE.—*Antioch.*
TIME.—A. D. 387.

SCENE I.—*The Market-place.*

Enter PAULUS *and* GLAUCUS.

Paul. Whence is this preacher whom the general voice
Declares a new Demosthenes?
Glau. 'Twas here
In Antioch his youthful years were spent;
Not heedlessly, like ours, but hovered o'er
With love and counsel, as with angel wings.
Like Samuel in the temple, he grew up
A priest; the robe his saintly mother wrought
Of pure example and of precepts wise
Investing him. Of older men he seemed
The natural ruler; but refused to wear
The name of bishop, and retired, when death
Had ended filial duty, to the cell
And cave. And now, as one who wandered far
To rob the hills and strain the streams of gold
Returns to spend his princely store, so he
Comes back to utter words so affluent
With wisdom and with grace, the multitude
Proclaim him CHRYSOSTOM, *the Golden Mouth.*

Paul. They say he deals with dialectics less
Than with the life?
Glau. Why yes, the chemistry
Of light, or what the difference precise
May be between the beams of sun and moon
Doth not so much concern his thought as that
The light may penetrate the world, to cheer,
Reprove and purify.
Paul. Amidst the throng
Whom this new Orpheus with his music charms
Are met, they say, the human butterflies
And bees who once to gather sweets, and air
Their robes of gauzy grace found full employ.
But strange above all else that Rumor tells
Is this: that Glaucus, gayest of the gay,
Forsakes full oft the theatre, the grove
Where dance the nymphs around Apollo's statue,
The chariot-race, and every scene that once
Enchanted him, to hear the homilies
That pour persuasion from the Golden Mouth.
Glau. For my apology hear him thyself.
Paul. I will, upon occasion fit; and bid
The giant who subdues you all o'erthrow
My hard and skeptic judgment if he can.
Glau. A giant not in stature, if in mind;
Nor are his words as blows to break the will,

But rather rays that melt the feelings, fire
The purpose, and consume the dross of self.
But yesterday the great assembly stood
Responsive to each glance his eye shot forth,
The changing thoughts that fell, like light and shade,
Upon his lips, or lent his voice its tone.

Paul. Pity such power were not employed to quell
The rising waves of mutiny, that now
Do join the earthquake and the dearth to mar
Our state and spoil our dream of peace.

Glau. This was the very upshot of the speech
He gave us yesterday: 'Forbear,' he said,
'The loud applauses fit for theatres;
But lend the meed I covet fervently:
Arrest the rioters—the idle mob
Of miscreants who supply for paltry pay
The noise that dancers and that demagogues
Delight in, and to whom the rude revolt,
The clamorous cry, the clash of arms are sport.
Say not, oh citizens, that prudence shuns
To make of these vile men sworn enemies.
The Baptist made an impious king his foe,
But prudent silence had been cowardice,
Than which the true man sooner chooses death.
Nor say *the matter is not mine*, as Cain

Cried out "Am I my brother's keeper?" Each
Is keeper to the rest, and all are bound
To keep the commonwealth from injury.
If you that hear would undertake the task
You should compel from Pagan and from Jew
The cry: "These Christians saved our capital!"
Nay, let one man be charged with holy zeal—
His influence alone shall change a city!'

Paul. I would the eloquence had wrought so well
That bonds and banishment had rid our streets
Of all the cursèd crew ill-fortune sends
To vex and do us harm. [*Enter* SOOTHSAYER.
What say the stars,
Whose eyes prophetic scan events to us
Yet unrevealed?

Sooth. Of late the omens all
Are full of ire; the planets move perturbed,
And every augury gives note of evil.
What wonder if the ancient gods do frown
When some new-fangled faith disputes their throne,
Destroys their altars, and instead of us,
Their ministers, admits an upstart race
Of Christian sorcerers and Jewish jugglers?
But hark! what sounds are these? Already seems
The car of retribution rolling near.
[*They retire. A mob enters.*

First Rioter. Throw down the statues, and treat them as you'd treat the men they stand for.

Second Rioter. Why then here goes my sledge-hammer against the portly legs of the Emperor, to bring him down from his airy grandeur, that he may make obeisance to his mother earth.

Third Rioter. Man and wife are one, they say. 'Tis fitting the Empress should share the fortunes of her high and mighty lord, as, no doubt, she has shared his counsels and has had a hand in laying these outrageous imposts upon us. [*Beats down the statue of the Empress.*] Your Majesty, how like you a lowly life? For fear the rest of your body should be scornful toward your battered and broken limbs, I'll proceed to deal a few blows promiscuously. Zeus! these magnates are made of stuff that almost defeats the force of iron.

Fourth Rioter. Next comes this brazen Governor, who, when we march to his mansion and implore that he will abate the tax, whines out that he is only a subordinate, and must do the bidding of the higher powers. Down with thee, tool of tyranny!

Ringleader. Clear the ground of the whole impertinent tribe set up here in the heart of your city to remind you that you are slaves.

Mob. Down with oppression!

Ringleader. Down with the taxes!

Mob. Down with aristocracy!

Ringleader. So far, well. Now make a circle and we'll have a song:

Said the Big Man who sits
  On the wonderful throne—
'Do you know, my dear spouse,
  That the silver is gone?
I'll send down to the South
  To those Antioch kine,
And supply the sad drouth
  From their udders so fine.'—
Wait awhile, little man, and we'll show you the trick
How the Antioch kine give their milkers a kick!

Said the woman—'My lord,
  Get enough now, I pray;
I've not had a new robe
  For a week and a day:
And those Antioch dogs
  Lean they may be and lame,
But in forests and bogs
  They'll find plenty of game.'—
Wait awhile, little woman, perhaps you are right,
But the Antioch dogs think their teeth made to bite!

Quoth the Governor—'Heu!
  'Tis a pitiful case:
I must fleece my poor subjects
  Or else lose my place;
But the Antioch sheep,

Though they bleat, must be sheared;
With the rich favor keep—
Nothing then need be feared.'—
Wait awhile, little man, you may witness some fun;
For the Antioch sheep think their legs made to run!

Quoth the princes—''Tis vain
To deny sober facts:
We were made just to rule
And the rest to be taxed.
And those Antioch mules
Are most handy and tough—
Only mind these two rules:
Starve and beat them enough.'
Wait awhile, little men, for when you say Go!
The tough Antioch mules may presume to say No!

Ringleader. It grows dark. I know of sundry piles of timber and rags that would burn well and give us light enough to see within the very walls where live the lofty ones whose *consciences* will not let them join the enterprize. How much sweeter the sound of that word *conscience* than of its synonyme—*cowardice.*

Mob. Give us torches and we'll illuminate.

[*They set on fire several dwellings of the rich, but are attacked by the military; some of the leaders are arrested, and quiet is restored.*]

Paul. I think we now may venture forth; the storm
That sent us here for shelter is o'erpast.

Sooth. Haply the shower is over; but the storm
Is just beginning: In the transient lull
Let us consult discretion and fly home.

SCENE II.—*Outside the church of Chrysostom. A multitude, among them* PAULUS *and* GLAUCUS.

Glau. We shall not get within the crowded walls:
But here his voice may reach us.

Paul. Listen now.

Chrys. I warned you, citizens—myself forewarned
By influence from above—in vain. A gang
Of aliens brought the pestilence of vice
To rage and ravage here. Unwise and weak,
We put them not in quarantine, and here
Behold we lie as men decreed to death.
Imperial wrath aroused may swoop with wings
Of war upon our city, and may fix
The talons of its vengeance in ourselves.
But I upbraid you not. I bid you prove
Repentance now by courage and by faith
That lifts the soul above tempestuous times.

I bid you hope. The Emperor, though quick
To anger, is not hard of heart. To him
Already flies our bishop, Flavian,
Whom years, and feebleness, and heavy cares
Would keep at home, but love for you impels
To try the argument with Majesty.
His holy countenance and snowy locks
Will plead; and in his voice will blend the tones
Of pathos and authority, till ire
Within the royal breast will yield to pity.
I bid you hope; for here may each and all
Address the MAJESTY on high, who turns
The hearts of kings, as streams that run not straight
From goal to goal but yield to many a check
And channel. See what cause for gratitude
Amidst our grief, for now no more the church
Is vacant, while the street is full; no more
The voice of sinful revelry confounds
Our songs of praise; nor seems the Sacred Word
An empty sound. As when a tempest broods
Dark o'er the deep the wandering craft take heed
And turn their prows and set their sails to seek
Safe harbor, till the roadstead void and still
Becomes a populous and vocal place,
While all the sea is desert—so the haunts
Of vice and idleness, the very marts

Of industry are left to solitude
And silence, while the sanctuary finds
Not room enough to hold its guests, and truth
Reverberates in every conscience. Now
There needs no tongue to tell the vanity
Of wealth ; for while the rich, distracted, run
To make some safe deposit of their goods,
The light-equipped are ready for the march.
Oh let the lesson live in memory ;
Nor think that gold can bribe the King of kings
And bid the day of dissolution welcome.
When prayers are answered and the peril past
Let not your hearts forget their vows and turn
Again to vanity.
Glau. The air is stifling :
Come, let us walk and talk together.—Well,
What thought you of our famous preacher, John ?
Paul. Of him I thought but little ; of the words
He uttered much and of the faith sublime
That animates his soul. The piety
That gives such triumph over trouble seems
Of priceless worth and sprung from truth divine.
Glau. 'Tis like my Paulus thus to speak, in spite
Of prejudice. I would that mine had been
The true translation of the word of Christ,
To teach my friend the way and truth and life.

Paul. Of late I saw and felt a something new
And not of earth, whene'er I met with thee.
The gayety was gone, but in its place
Appeared such tranquil joy and purity
As if a babbling, effervescent rill
Had lost itself within the bosom broad
And deep of some bright lake wherein the heaven
Doth look to see another heaven.—What means
This noise of wailing and of prayer that grows
More loud as we approach the Hall of Justice?

Glau. The judges whom the Emperor deputes
To find the fountain-head of mutiny
Sit daily in the Hall, to try with words
And tortures all who are accused, or whom
They reckon cognizant of the affair.
The great and small, the rich and poor are seized
And held in durance; while, without the court,
A crowd of sad petitioners pour forth
Their tearful lamentations and their prayers.

[*Enter Officers.*

First Officer. In the name of Theodosius, Emperor, we arrest you for treason.

Glau. and Paul. We are no traitors.

Second Officer. Ha! you cannot skulk under a lie as you skulked in the shadow of the arcade, after taking part in a high-handed outrage. A few turns of the screw will be likely to quicken your memories and squeeze out of your lips a little truth.

Second Officer. Along with you!

Glau. A better One than we, and for our sake,
Endured the lot of shame and suffering:
The thought of Him shall bring relief to pain.

[*They are taken into the Hall. Enter the street on horseback the judges; a company of monks, with Macedonius at their head, meeting them.*]

Mac. Alight, oh servants of an earthly lord,
And hear the mandates of the Lord of heaven!

Cæs. If with the sword and spear thou didst presume
To stay our progress, or didst use the name
Of human potentate to give thy word
Authority, the answer should be made
Of scorn and steel; but in thy coarse attire
And wasted form and sanctity of mien
We recognize supreme prerogative.

[*They dismount.*

Mac. Suspend the sword; and bid your sovereign think
Although a master he is but a man;
And those whom he arrests are men, whom God
Hath made in his own image. If, to break
The brazen statue of the Emperor

Be criminal, what greater crime to break
Remorselessly the living statue formed
In likeness of the Lord! A little gold
Will mould again the now demolished brass,
But with what price shall grief restore the lives
That rash revenge so easily destroyed?

Cæs and *Helleb.* Your words are oracles, and till they reach
The royal ears and bring response, our work
Shall have an intermission.

Mac. Pax vobiscum. [*Exeunt.*

SCENE III.—*The Church on the morning of Easter.*

Enter Bishop FLAVIAN, CHRYSOSTOM, PAULUS, GLAUCUS *and people.*

Chrys. When o'er us hung the heavy clouds of fear
I bade you praise the Lord, the ever good,
Nor suffer faith to fail. The clouds are past;
The skies are full of cheer! As when the hearts
That seemed but dead and sepulchred with Christ

With him arose, rejoicing over death,
So, on this Easter morn, our spirits spring
Elastic from the darkness into light.
When first the hand of retribution fell,
The great and rich—in other days so proud
And potent—thought alone of speedy flight
And safety for their goods: but men unknown,
Unarmed and poor, save for their faith in God,
Made haste to bring us help; they stayed our doom,
Then vanished back from unfamiliar scenes
To their accustomed hills and trees and caves.
As angels came they, and as angels went.
And now returns, to crown our festival,
The shepherd who, to save his flock, deemed not
His own life dear, but braved the boisterous seas,
The wintry cold, the Emperor's kindled wrath.
As Moses pleaded, 'Save the people, LORD,
Or let me perish with them!' So hath he,
Our father Flavian, implored for us;
And not in vain; he brings this royal letter:

[*Reads.*]

'The Lord of worlds for our sake took the form of a servant; and for those who nailed him to the cross he prayed: "Father, forgive them!" What great thing is it if they who are mere men forgive the injuries inflicted by those who are their fellow-servants? The Emperor freely pardons the offences of his Antioch subjects, in the hope that his clemency may not be lost upon them and that he himself may find mercy with the Supreme Monarch. THEODOSIUS, Emperor.'

[*Outbreak of joy.*]

Let gratulation rise to gratitude
And fill the numbers of our Easter hymn.

HYMN.

We sing of a Saviour ascended.
On earth once our sorrows he bore;
But the shame and the grief are now ended,
He shall reign and rejoice evermore.
Hallelujah let us sing!
Not sweet spices for the dead
But the palm and sceptre bring,
Crown the King and Conqueror's head!

He hath broken death's ancient dominion;
'Tis no longer a terror to die.
With the strength of his sky-piercing pinion
Our hopes he hath lifted on high.
Praise the Lord of life and light!
Lo an empty tomb is here;
Where the Christ hath winged his flight
All that love him shall appear.

He has gone to his Capital splendid
Not as one might the conflict forsake,
But that we, by his succors befriended,
May in warfare his triumph partake.

Praise the source of strength and grace,
  Rich in mercy, clothed with power!
Though we see not now his face
  He is with us every hour.

When the forces of nature do mutiny,
  When around us are riot and rage,
When God's law bids us quail 'neath its scrutiny,
  He our sorrow and dread doth assuage.
    For the quiet of our state,
      For the quelling of our fear,
    For our hope and joy elate
      Sing we hallelujahs here!

III.

PERSONS REPRESENTED.

CHRYSOSTOM.
EUTROPIUS, *Prime Minister.*
EUDOXIA, *Empress.*
OLYMPIAS, *A deaconess.*

SCENE.—*Constantinople.*
TIME.—A. D. 398.

SCENE I.—*Room in the Royal Palace.*

Enter EUTROPIUS *and* EUDOXIA.

Eut. My pretty Empress, I have caught and caged
For thee a singing bird whose fluent notes—
Albeit sometimes sharp and shrill—might move
The envy of the Attic groves. Commend
Thy servant's zeal and make his gift right welcome.

Eud. Arch plotter, what new feat hast thou accomplished?

Eut. Oh nothing to be named beside the feat
That won me reputation.

Eud. What was that?

Eut. To teach an orphan maiden, young and fair,
Her place upon a height imperial;
To teach an Emperor her charms to choose
In place of hers to whom he was betrothed—
The daughter of his Minister, Rufinus;
And when the proud Prime Minister returned
From Antioch, flushed with hope which he had bought
By bloodshed—when the wedding-day was come
And all the city blossomed forth in joy,
And myriad eyes, half-dazed with splendor, turned

Expectant toward the great Rufinus' house—
To pass that stately mansion by, and bear
The royal gifts within Eudoxia's door,
And lead her forth, with her own beauty crowned,
Amidst the chorus of a populace
Admiring and amazed; and so to see
The orphan queen of more than half the world!
Live I an age and with invention vex
My days and nights, never another prize
So rich shall compensate my pains.

Eud. My lord,
You do yourself injustice when you place
This vaunted exploit highest on your list.

Eut. Why what could higher stand?

Eud. To take a slave
Whom masters could not keep, and whom at last
An officer bestowed upon his daughter
As one whose cunning hand was fit to braid
Her flowing tresses and to dress her head;
To take this deft and dangerous chattel out
From bondage and advance him, step by step,
Till he should reach a round o'erlooking all
The lords and princes of the land—nay more,
Should make the throne itself subordinate,
Enact the policy, and sell for gold
The offices in all the realm, depose,

Imprison and confiscate, at his will—
To him who wrought this marvel I award
The meed of genius unapproachable!
Eut. Your majesty is pleased to flatter me.
Eud. Do I not know what wily purpose planned
To make me Majesty? Rufinus, foul
With murder of my guardian, was my foe:
If I should rise then he must fall; and thou
By lifting me shouldst win the vacancy.
Because my face was fair and fortune smiled
The scheme succeeded: I am Empress; thou
Prime Minister; Rufinus—
Eut. Stay, I like
Not well to hear of him.
Eud. 'Tis certain quite
That *from* him thou wilt never hear, unless
Dead men return to life. The daughter must,
If still she lives, admire thee much!
Eut. A truce.
Why do you not inquire about my bird?
Eud. Your bird indeed! He wears a golden name
And waits to wear the plumage of a bishop.
I heard to-day of his arrival here.
Eut. Not willingly did Antioch give her son,
To grace the grand metropolis; and he
Was proof against persuasion: but the men

We sent had orders absolute to bring
Him hither, though by stratagem or force.
A message summoned him outside the town,
And there a carriage waited. Thrust within,
His angry questions Why? and Whither? met
A bland but blind response, till far away
The city had receded—left to learn
Its loss upon the morrow, when the ship
That bore our bishop should her sails expand
To reach the port that never knew a peer.
Eud. 'Twas managed cleverly; and we will make
The captive so contented he shall sing
His sweetest notes. No music to my ear
So pleasing as the eloquence inspired
By sacred truth. Besides, I do confess
Our worldly, venal priesthood need the curb
This rigid hand will ply. Tell him, at once,
The Emperor and I must welcome him.
How, think you, will the proud Theophilus,
Of Alexandria, bear to see a man
Like this made Metropolitan, in place
Of one compliant whom he might employ
To serve his plans at court?
Eut. 'Twill vex him sore.
Bid him attend the consecration here:
If he refuse to come, or to confirm

The rite, I know a method magical
To break his stubborn will.
Eud. What is the magic?
Eut. A certain passage of his history,
Recorded on a parchment, which divulged
Would serve his honors like a sudden frost
That makes the shining leaf a faded rag.
Eud. What should I do without Eutropius?
[*Exit* EUT.
And yet I tremble lest his love of gold
And power should teach him treachery to me.

SCENE II.—*Room in the Bishop's Palace*—CHRYSOSTOM *at study.*

Enter a priestly attendant.

Att. Olympias, who serves the church so well,
Desires to see thee.
Chrys. Stay, till thou hast told,
More perfectly than I have learned as yet
Her character and life.
Att. Of noble birth
And rich and beautiful, she early knew
An orphan's lot, but learned from Christian lips

The law of piety ; and when, alas,
A brief-time bride, bereavement broke her heart,
'Twas even like the breaking of the box
Of alabaster at the Master's feet :
For all her store of wealth and richer store
Of love were made an offering to the Lord,
And with the fragrance of her holy life
And kindly deeds the region round was filled.
The Emperor Theodosius thought her mad
To make such sacrifice while yet so young ;
And that her property might bide the time
Of her recovery, he locked it fast
Beneath a guardian's key. Her ready thanks
For such relief as left her free to run
With lightsome step along the heavenly path,
His purpose changed : he gave the treasures back.
Which she received indifferent, like some peak
Aloft that takes the clouds, not drinking them
But sending lavish currents down to drench
The thirsty lowlands. Others idly feast
And flourish on her gifts ; her garb is coarse
Her fare is meagre and her life a cross.
Our church has not another minister
Who serves with self-denial so intense.

Chrys. The church makes men of women ; while
the world

Makes women those who should be men. The fops
Who promenade with painted cheeks, curled locks
And leer of license, give you these the name
That signifies self-rule and courage, strength
To do and suffer? 'Twere profanity!
We'll call the weaklings *women* if the word
Be not too pure and dignified. And they
Who in a woman's body bear a heart
So stout the devil cannot conquer it,
Nor fear of death nor tortures such as those
The mother of the Macabees endured
When in her presence all her sons were slain—
Oh call them *men* if in that word is power
To tell what virtue grace divine bestows
Upon the weak. In Hebrew times there lived
A race of manly women; on the steps
Of Christ and Paul such women waited, true
When trusted men were false. Thank God He gives
Us here such helpers. Bid Olympias come.

[*Enter* OLYMPIAS.

I greet thee as a woman whom the Lord
In love hath led to choose the better part.

Olym. To thee I yield the reverence due to one
Who fills with holy zeal a holy office.
If all were like thee! But alas, the crime
Of that bad king in Persia's capital

Who in the golden chalices that once
Had served Jehovah's temple drank the wine
Of wassail,is repeated oft by men
Who make their priesthood servant of their sin.
Thy predecessor here, Nectarius,
Too fond of gain and luxury himself,
Gave not good heed to his subordinates.
I would not censure ; but thy light hath made
The dark appear more palpable and sad.

Chrys. Lady, I prize thy praise but need thy prayers :
Myself a man imperfect, set to rule
O'er men of envy, fickleness and greed.
The indolent resent our call to prayer
That steals an hour from sleep ; the covetous
Lament their revenues reduced to build
A hospital for strangers ; and the lax
In morals hate the hand that would restrain.
The church scarce more alive than dead—the court
Corrupt—society a pestilence—
What wonder if I sometimes cry with him
Who prophesied in old Jerusalem :
'Oh that my head were waters and mine eyes
A fount of tears that I might weep the slain
By day and night.' Amidst applause I preach
To those who gather in the house of God

With vain display of robes and retinue,
And who depart the place to find
New entertainment at the games, where oft
With folly meet debauchery and shame.
I would I were once more an eremite
Amidst the wilds, less rude to me than pomp
And vice in Constantine's proud capital!
Olym. Flee not, like Jonah, from the call of God
Who bids thee to this Nineveh proclaim
His messages of mercy and of woe.
Nor think thy work in vain: already rise
A multitude to call thee blessed. More
And more the bad shall fear thee and the good
Be comforted.
Chrys. Forgive the fretfulness
That courts reproof from kindly lips like thine.
I will resume my office and inquire
What service I may render thee.
Olym. My friend
And father, I would lay on thee the load
That wealth inherited hath laid on me.
At once relieve my anxious thought and rid
My conscience of a snare: for vanity
Full oft, with cunning malice, whispers me:
What merit in thy large beneficence!
As statues stand the chu ches thou hast built,

The hospitals by thee endowed. Thy gifts
To rich and poor are destined to embalm
Thy memory. Help me to wrest away
This weapon from the fiendish hand that fain
Would slay my soul.
Chrys. Thy talent is thine own,
To use but not transfer. In open fight,
And not evasively, thy soul must win
Its amaranthine wreath of victory.
Olym. Why then, if thou decline the proffered trust
I'll make all comers free to take the store
Of wealth that cumbers me, till all is gone.
Chrys. 'I was an hungered and ye gave me food,
Was naked and ye clothed me:' how shall Christ
Address such words to thee if carelessly
Thou give to those who have enough, and lose
Thereby the power to help the destitute?
Olm. I had not thought of that, but of the scorn
Which piety should put on earthly goods.
Chrys. 'With earthly mammon win a heavenly home,'
The Master saith. Full soon the tent will fall
That gives thy too impetuous spirit shelter,
And thou wilt need the friends thy charity
Hath made, to welcome thee within

An everlasting and celestial house.

Olym. As if an angel spake I hear thy words :
Oh teach me alway what is right.
Farewell.

[*Exit* OLYMPIAS.

Chrys. [*To attendant.*] If ever thou incline to lose thy faith
In human virtue or in heavenly grace
I bid thee think of her and such as she.

Att. I do not doubt thy words to her were wise ;
But if she follow them and scant the gifts
That make the rich more rich, resentment vile
Will couple scandal with her name and thine.
'Tis history inspires the prophecy.

Chrys. I will not think ingratitude so base
That it can wrong a saint like her unsullied.

Att. Heaven justify thy generous unbelief!

IV.

PERSONS REPRESENTED.

CHRYSOSTOM, EUTROPIUS, EUDOXIA, OLYMPIAS,
ARCADIUS, *Emperor.*
Attendant and Officer.

SCENE.—*Constantinople.*
TIME.—A. D. 400.

SCENE I.—*Room in the Royal Palace.*

Enter ARCADIUS *and* EUTROPIUS.

Eut. This traitor, Tribigild, with all his Goths,
From Phrygia is moving like a cloud
Of wrath; and Gainas whom we sent to stay
The storm augments it, joining force to force.

Arc. They send a messenger to bring the terms
Of their withdrawal hence in amity.

Eut. I know the terms proposed: Betray thy friend;
Consent to be a ruler but in name,
While ruffians and barbarians usurp
The true authority; in place of me,
Accept the minister they nominate,
And thou shalt have their pledge of peace—a pledge
Whose worth is weighty as their honor is!
Make haste to seize the bait, forgetting risk
Of future vengeance from a man whose wit
Hath made and may unmake a monarch's fortune.

Arc. Content. Prime Minister thou shalt remain
Though devils join the foes that plot thy fall.

Eut. There speaks an Emperor. My deeds shall tell
My gratitude. What man can do will I.

[*Exit* EUTROPIUS. *Enter military officer.*

Off. Your Majesty, the frantic populace
Are surging at the palace gates. They cry
'Down with Eutropius! Give the worthless slave
To be an offering for the nation's life!'

[*Enter* EUDOXIA, *leading her two children.*

Eud. The peril is most imminent! Without,
A horde of heathen congregate in arms;
Infuriate rebellion rocks the city.
And here, within our residence, we keep
The guilty cause of our calamity.
By all the loyalty a nation claims
From thee, its head; by all thy love of life
And regal state; by all the argument
The helplessness of children can address
To move a father's heart, and by the vows
That made thee mine, to cherish and defend me,
I do implore thee give Eutropius up
To sate the raging appetite of vengeance.

Arc. I thought thou didst regard him as a friend.

Eud. I feared him, and I felt his subtle skill
To fascinate whom he would make his prey:
But lately he has grown so insolent

Of manner and his speech so menacing,
I hail the tempest that may shake him off—
The fire wherein this viper may be burned.

Arc. My word is pledged to keep him safe from harm.

Eud. Oh, thou hast pledges earlier and more sacred.
Behold the partner of thy throne falls down
A suppliant at its footstool, and her tears,
So hot with love's intensity that ice
Would be inflamed beneath them, urge my suit,
And, moved by sympathy and fear, these babes
With bitter cry appeal to thee for help.

Arc. Arise; I am a man, not adamant
Nor metal to resist such melting pleas.
Eutropius must die, unless for him
Escape should open from the frenzied mob
And unrelenting soldiers to the place
Where fugitives, though tracked by justice, find
Security.

Eud. Behold the meet reward
Of cruelty and crime! The ancient law
Of sanctuary was contemned by him
Who fain would find asylum now beneath
The altar of the house of God; and when
Our holy bishop would not yield the lives

This impious slave desired, thy hand was moved
To sign the law's repeal. The door is shut!
For him who showed no mercy there remains
No mercy more. [*To the officer.*

Arc. Assure the citizens
That their demands shall meet compliance. So
May peace return to our distracted state. [*Exeunt.*

SCENE II.—*The Cathedral.*

EUTROPIUS *at the Altar.* CHRYSOSTOM *discoursing from the pulpit to the people.*

I bade you write on all things *vanity*;
On beauty, splendor, wealth and noisy fame.
But in the peaceful, prosperous days my words
Were lost, like arrows shot into the sea.
Lo here a sermon superseding all
My lips would say. The tree that flourished fair
Is stripped of leaves and stands a naked trunk.
Where is the light that blazed refulgent round
The courtier's steps? Where now the cheers that rang
Whene'er the race-course or the theatre
Was graced and gladdened by his presence? Where
The friends who wafted praises to his power

As incense to a god? It was a dream!
The light has dawned, the vapor vanishes!

[*To* EUTROPIUS.

Oh man, I mock thee not, but cite thee here
A witness for the truth. Thou hadst an idol:
Invoke thine idol, money, now to save thee.
Alas, it would have murdered thee. The church
Thou didst revile, its ministry didst menace;
Its altars thou didst seek to bar against
Misfortune and misdeed: the first to seek
Forbidden shelter is thyself! Race-course
And theatre which thou didst patronize
Resound the cry: Give up the wretch to death!
Thy boon companions are thine enemies:
Thy friends are they who felt thy biting scorn:
Thy safe asylum is the hated church.
Oh hadst thou heeded wisdom's voice! but now
Thou liest abject and undone.
Kind friends,
The world's defeat is triumph to Christ's church.
Her glory is to shield the weak, whate'er
The hostile forces that encompass them.
The people, Emperor and army stand
Arrayed against this cunning criminal:
Be ours the task to turn their rage to pity.
Say not that penitence will not suffice

To cleanse the guilt of his rapacity;
Say not his touch pollutes the sacred altar.
A sinner washed the Saviour's feet unblamed.
And who is he can pray '*Father forgive
As I forgive*,' while harboring revenge?
Come, while I seek the Emperor, implore
With humble hearts the King who reigns supreme
That He will give this trophy to our altar.
[*Clamor of troops without, crying, 'Surrender the robber! Give him up, or we will raze the house to the ground.'*]
Be not affrighted, for the Lord is here:
The ship that Jesus sails in cannot sink.

SCENE III.—*A Room in Olympias' House.*

Olym. How like a solitude the city seems
Since Chrysostom is absent. As, if rain
Or sunshine be withdrawn, the earth grows sad
And sere, though all the elements beside
Fulfil their functions—we that serve with him
Do thirst and droop until his beaming face
Return and on our hearts the showers shall fall
Of his refreshing eloquence. We chide

The zeal that bade him brave the boisterous seas
And penetrate the camp of barbarous men.
And yet how noble and how like himself!
For vile Eutropius he was moved to plead,
Till death, decreed, gave place to banishment:
No wonder that for those who well had served
The state but whom the angry Goths had doomed
To die, his dauntless heart should prompt this deed
Of dangerous enterprise. HAND that dost hold
The deep and hold the souls of men—kind HEART
That dost regard our sad solicitude—
MIND that dost plan the welfare of Thy church,
Oh give the faithful pastor sure defence;
Make Thou his mission prosperous; give him
The lives for which his own he perils; bring
The wanderer safely, surely home! 'Tis well
These walls are trusty; else my meditations,
My very prayers, if breathed aloud, would be,
To men impure and envious, my accusers.
Oh evil and ungrateful days, when vows
Of consecration, witnessed by a life
Of self-denying zeal, impose no check
On slander. Oh ignoble souls that make
The purest friendship but a vulgar love,
As waters dull and darkened do display
A dull and darkened picture of the sky.

[*Enter Attendant.*

Att. Madame, our bishop is come home and brings
From Tribigild and Gainas pardon free
To them who wrought no wrong but whom revenge
For justice done by them condemned to death.

Olym. The news is pleasant and I thank thee for it.

Att. I thought thou wouldst have clapped thy hands and cried
For joy, when even I, who know him less,
Was half beside myself with ecstasy.

Olym. We must not suffer feeling to o'erflow
The bounds of safe sobriety, nor fail
In joyful times to think how soon some grief
May follow and consume our joy.

Att. To pour
Away the sparkling foam from fortune's cup
And let the liquor cool before I quaffed it
I should not like.

Olym. We will not quarrel, child;
Go you and join the general concourse; give
The holy man my greeting. I will see him soon.

Att. [*aside.*] She should have welcomed him at once,
With her own lips, and not with mine instead, [*Exit.*

Olym. Now, grateful heart, teach thou my lips to sing,

Till prudence shall release my tethered steps
And give me leave, unblamed by jealous eyes,
To look upon my father and my friend.

From the wilderness and wave,
  From the hosts of armèd men,
He who went the doomed to save
  Safe himself returns again.
          Welcome him!

Rich and potent, whom his voice
  Warns of peril, tells of peace,
Wins to make the better choice—
  Rank and wealth that ne'er will cease—
          Welcome him!

Ye that pine in poverty,
  Ye that feel oppression's rod,
Hail your helper joyfully;
  With thanksgivings unto God
          Welcome him!

Flock, for whom the shepherd cares
  With a thoughtful, constant love,
For his toils and tears and prayers
  With the glad procession move;
          Welcome him!

Chosen sharers of his joy,
  Of his labor and his grief,
As ye prize the high employ
  In his greeting be ye chief;
          Welcome him!

V.

PERSONS REPRESENTED.

CHRYSOSTOM, PAULUS, FLAVIAN, GLAUCUS, OLYMPIAS.
THEODORA, *a Deaconess.*
Bishops, Officers and Messengers.

SCENE.—*Cônstantinople and neighborhood.*
TIME.—A. D. 403.

SCENE I.—*Room in the Bishop's Palace.*

Enter CHRYSOSTOM, PAULUS *and* FLAVIAN.

Chrys. [*To Paulus.*] To look upon thee is to see again
My native city with its hills surrounded;
The river winding through; the long arcade,
With marble paved, with people dense; the church
Where first I found my voice and felt the thrill
Of thoughts enkindled by the listening throng.
It is to live again the years of youth,
Whose memory is tender as the light
Of evening or the notes of distant music.
Where is the youth we loved—to me a son,
To you a brother and a guide?

Paul. You speak
Of Glaucus? He who sometime trod
The treacherous ways of pleasure numbers now
His prayers within the hollow mountain side,
And makes his hermitage the haunt of thoughts
As high above this sensual earth as are
The paths of eagles over sordid dust.

Chrys. A blessed choice—the company of God
And peace, in lieu of uproar and the strife
With wicked men! Why was it not thine own?
Paul. I sought indeed the solitude, but felt
An impulse such as sent Saint Christopher
To seek some active labor that might serve
His God. Not mine, like his, a giant's strength;
Yet haply might I ferry o'er the flood
Some feeble pilgrim to the promised land.
And therefore am I come, in hope that he
Who first my errant footsteps led aright
Will show me now the work that waits for me,
And teach me how I may perform it well.
And Flavian, who in Rome the pearl of price
Obtained, from Alexandrian schools resorts
To thee for wisdom and authority,
To help the triumph of the sacred cause.
Chrys. I greet you as my brethren much beloved.
'The harvest fields are white, the laborers few:'
From far Phœnicia, with its idol groves,
From barbarous Goths among the German wilds,
From multitudes of heathen here at home,
And half-instructed, faltering followers
Of Christ, the Macedonian message comes.
Oh were an apostolic zeal the mark
Of all who bear the name of laborers!

Alas, the idle and the covetous
Encumber even our too slender ranks.
Fla. We would be taught what arguments to use
With unbelieving and with wayward men.
Chrys. All other arguments are weak and vain
Beside the logic of a holy life.
The eloquence of speech is mean compared
With that of conduct. Lo, 'the heavens are still
But they declare the glory of the Lord.'
Even to them point not as witnesses,
But to the new creation wrought in Christ
Who sets discordant souls in harmony,
Fills all their faculties with holy light,
And lifts, above the low and changeful earth,
A radiant and immortal heaven of hope.
Not, if your gifts were miracles—to still
The storm or raise the dead—were ye so armed
As with consistency. For that which calms
The rage of passion and dissolves the spell
That binds the ethereal spirit in the dust
Doth demonstrate itself as most divine.
Let proud refinement, with its rhetoric,
Pronounce apostles and evangelists
Unfit for seats among philosophers,
And men of classic lore. A rustic sling,
The pebble picked from out the running brook,

In David's hand o'erthrew the giant proud
For all his jointed mail and ponderous shield.
Celestial power, that nerved the stripling's arm,
More plain appeared because the means were small.
And Christian truth, that in the forehead smites
Iniquity, proclaims itself from God
By reason of its very artlessness.
Its weakness is its strength; its shame its glory.
Oppose malevolence and hate with love:
The deed of love shall give truth's word effect
That else were lost, like rain upon a rock.
Love is the power deific that can make
Of stony hearts the children of our God.
Spread its fine net to catch the souls astray:
Lest with the weapons of rebuke and scorn
You scare them into regions far remote,
Forever wandering and forever lost.

Paul. What shall we say to those who measure faith
By rigid rules of reason, and deny
Whate'er is broad or high beyond the range
Of human comprehension?

Chrys. Say that faith
Is propped by reason, but hath wings to soar
Above it, as imagination hath

To leave the mathematic bounds of sense.
And say that he who will not worship save
A God whom reason comprehendeth well
Must idolize mere matter or mankind.
Only the spirit in us worshippeth
The Spirit infinite.
Paul. And what to those
Who call themselves 'the pure' and bid the guilty,
When once they hear the church's censure, seek
Her altar nevermore, though penitent?
Chrys. Say that a sea without a wave to wash
The shore were less a wonder than a soul
Without a sin; that they account themselves
More pure than Paul who styled himself 'the chief
Of sinners,' and forget the Master's word:
'Till seven times seventy if thy brother sin
And turn again repentantly, forgive.'
But leave the lesson here. I would inquire
What tidings Flavian from the Orient brings;
For dire disasters, flying thence, o'ercloud
And threaten us. Theophilus, whom I
Forgave for envy, caught in tricks of fraud,
Raves and invents revenge on every side,
Like some huge monster of the deep that, mad
With wounds, the water lashes into foam.
The monks, who in the Nitrian desert dwelt

At peace, because their leaders dared refuse
Connivance with his knavery feel his wrath;
The charge of heresy is hotly hurled
Upon them; fire and plunder spoil their home:
The sword pursues them into Palestine,
And to the shore where eighty men embark
In hope to find a refuge and redress
With us. Could I their piteous plea withstand?
I wrote in tears to beg Theophilus
Would take the offenders back. For answer came
A deputation to incriminate
The monks. In turn, they charged Theophilus
With crimes: and when I would have stayed their
purpose
They sought the Empress and implored her help.
Her heart of tenderness and piety
Was touched. She promised; and forthwith a court
Was summoned—I the judge; Theophilus,
My brother bishop, the arraigned.—Heard you
At home so much? [*To Flavian.*

Fla. And more than this I heard:
The angry hierarch declares aloud
Constantinople shall receive him soon,
But not as one who meets a culprit charge;
The tables shall be turned, and *thou* shalt stand
Thy trial at *his* judgment-seat.

Chrys. 'Tis well;
I would not be his judge—I fear him not
As mine.
Paul. Integrity is void of fear;
But enemies can make the fairest life
Look infamous. Thine enemies are many:
The rich whose avarice thou hast rebuked,
The priests corrupt whom thou hast dared depose,
And one whose power the throne acknowledges.
Chrys. The pious Empress?
Paul. Ay, her piety
Delights itself in churchly rites and gifts;
Aud thus she veils her cruelty and greed.
As Herod hated John she hates the man
Whom royalty nor forms of sanctity
Can blind to sin.
Chrys. The words seem harsh, and yet
They match too well the deeds that late have moved
My sad surmise.
Paul. Heaven fend from thee all harm!
But if affliction come, give us but leave
To share it with thee.
Chrys. God be with you both.

SCENE II.—*A street.*

Enter PAULUS *and* GLAUCUS, *meeting.*

Paul. What eye could recognize the Spring-time tree—
With all its wealth of leaf and song and flower—
When Autumn ashes cover it? And yet
The face emaciate in this solemn cowl
Brings back to memory one who sported erst
His colors gay, and sang with gleeful voice.

Glau. I had forgotten him.

Paul. But not thy friend?

Glau. Oh no, and least of all the friend who found
With me the Best of friends.

Paul. And may I know
What brings thee from thine aerie down to tread
The dusty level of this noisy world?

Glau. The sounds are sifted that ascend toward us:
The notes of common strife and grief and mirth
Fall heavy to the ground from which they sprung;
But sometimes, clear and loud as midnight bells,
The voices of events do call to us.

And then—as angels, less of earth than we,
Have visited the rude abodes of men—
We leave the silent solitudes, the air
And light that lave the upper realm, to mix
Once more in scenes renounced. The summons
came
To me when one I love and venerate
Was brought beneath the scourge of lying tongues,
And menaced with the forfeiture of life.
Our Lord Himself in sorrow's heavy hour
Would feel assured that faithful friends were nigh:
And who to Chrysostom should comfort bring
But we who to his holy teachings owe
Our comfort here and hope of heavenly life?
Paul. A goodly company assemble now
Within his residence. Go we at once
To join our sympathy with theirs.
Glau. What course
Already hath the scheme nefarious run?
Paul. Of many strands a cunning cord is wove,
To bind the faithful bishop where his work
And words will no more rouse the jealousy
Of rivals, nor the wrath of wicked men.
Within the dwelling of Eugraphia,
Whose dress indecorous had drawn the fire
Of censure from his lips, a conclave met

Of all the malcontents : the venal priests,
The hireling courtiers and the spiteful dames.
Imperial favor helped to hatch the plot.
When all is ready comes Theophilus,
A train of cleric pomp attending him.
In yon Chalcedon he hath fixed his quarters :
But daily to and fro, between the town
And suburb, swift this spider runs and spins
His web. At last within *The Oak*—a church
So named, near by Chalcedon—sits the court :
The long indictment is unrolled and read.
Oh wonderful ! The snows of Lebanon
Are blamed for blackness, and the light of heaven
Indicted for misleading men !

Glau. What mean you ?

Paul. Of heresy, of falsehood and of fraud,
Of blasphemy, and gluttony and strife
Is he accused whose life-blood seems composed
Of self-denial, purity and peace !—
Here is the bishop's house beside the church.

SCENE III.—*Hall in the palace of the Bishop. A large company of ecclesiastics present and weeping.*

Enter PAULUS *and* GLAUCUS.

Chrys. What mean ye, friends, to weep and break
my heart?
'For me to live is Christ; to die is gain.'
This world is but a market-place wherein
We meet to buy and sell, and then go home.
Think not the Master will forget his church
Or fail to furnish helpers for her need.
In God, the Lord, forevermore rejoice.
[*Enter deputation from Council.*
With honors due your ranks I do salute
The legates of the sacerdotal Council.

Messenger. [*Reads.*] '*The Holy Synod of the Oak to John: We have received charges against thee of a thousand crimes; therefore, appear and answer.*'

Bishop Sallust. We deny that Theophilus has any lawful jurisdiction in this diocese.

Bishop Serapion. He himself refused, on like

grounds, to appear at the citation of John: wherefore, if he is ready to correct his reading of the canon, it behooves him to take the place of the accused in this presence; for ours is as legal a tribunal as that which is set up at Chalcedon.

Chrys. The jurisdiction I indeed deny,
But will defend myself before the court,
If only they who are my enemies,
By word and deed pronounced, shall sit no more
Among my judges to discolor truth.

[*Enter officer of the Crown.*

Off. [*Reads*] '*Hereby the Emperor orders the Bishop John to obey the summons of the Holy Synod and stand his trial at The Oak.* —ARCADIUS.

Chrys. The Emperor cannot unmake the right
Of the arraigned to claim a trial fair;
And not for forty orders will I go,
Except by force, to let my honor fall
A prey to malice, under forms of law.

Egyptian Bishops. We have an answer ready for this bold and blasphemous declaration; The Council has decreed, that if the accused fail to appear he shall be adjudged guilty, deposed from office and committed to the Imperial power for the punishment due to high treason.

Friends of Chrysostom. To the church! To the church!

[*They move into the church adjoining. Chrysostom ascends the pulpit and addresses the multitude who assemble.*

Chrys. The waves run high, the mighty floods are out!
Yet fear we not; the Rock is under us.
Of what should true believers be afraid?
Of death? Their Saviour lives, and they with him.
Of banishment? The wide world is the Lord's.
Of loss of goods? We nothing brought with us,
And nothing can we carry forth from life.
Good friends, be full of courage and of hope!
Our souls no death nor distance can divide,
Nor can assaults Satanic shake the church.
Her ancient foes forgotten, while she lives—
Her wall shall stand against the present shock
Unweakened, while the men that seek her harm
Shall perish. Mine is not an idle boast;
I have the pledge of Christ—his note of hand:
'Where two or three are met am I.' And this:
'Lo, I am with you till the world shall end.'
The Rock of Ages will resist the plots
And powers of hell. Exult and praise the Lord!
So shall you comfort me, who, for your sake,

Would die a thousand deaths, nor count it more
Than duty from the shepherd to his flock.

A voice in the crowd. A more than mortal courage animates him. Let us organize a guard, and, night and day, defend this sacred house from the violence of those who would rob the poor of their benefactor, and religion of its ablest advocate and best representative.

All. Agreed! Agreed! Let us organize!

SCENE IV.—*The sea-shore below the city. A multitude: among whom* OLYMPIAS *and* THEODORA.

Theo. The sun, that seemed forever swallowed up
In clouds, with sudden splendor dazzles us.
Say, will he keep his prosperous course henceforth,
Or soon again be lost to us unhappy?

Olym. Alike in honor and in defamation
In wealth and poverty, our Chrysostom
Hath sung the self-same strain of *Praise to God;*
And many a soul hath caught from him the song

Unlearned before. I tremble lest on one
So patient and so pure, so full of love
And thankfulness vicissitude should try
Its full experiment. A jubilee
Awaits him now; to-morrow mockery
And violence may drive him forth. My fears
Make discord in the anthem of my heart.

Theo. The crowd increases, and the port doth deck
Its dancing masts with flags and pennons bright.
A thousand hands a thousand torches grasp
That of the night will make another day.
The children come with garlands, and the bands
Are ready with their most melodious mirth.
Upon the topmost summit of the tower
The watchman gazes seaward, if afar
He may descry the longed-for sail.

[*Enter* FLAVIAN.

Fla. [*To Olympias.*] Lady,
Well met. I bore thy benefactions large
To those whom famine threatened, and I bring
A heavier load of thanks from them to thee.

Olym. Thou must consent to bear a burden still:
For weighty thanks are due to one who braved
The desert and the flood, that he might feed
A starving people. Gladly would we hear
At once the story of the expedition.

Fla. Another day; for now I thirst to know
The meaning of this scene. On every side
I ask, and get this only answer back:
'Our Chrysostom comes home to-night!' I left
A city that was sad, a church whose doors
Were sealed and guarded to defend the man
For whom the city now makes festival.
Olym. Three days within the holy house he dwelt;
But when he heard that men in arms were sent
To apprehend him, forth, by secret ways,
He passed and gave himself into their hands.
By night—fit darkness for dark deed—they bore
The prisoner to the ship that o'er the sea
Was wafted to Prænetus. Rid of him,
His foes with loud invectives filled the air.
But, as a conflagration draws the clouds,
Their fury wrought reaction and resistance:
Tumultuous debate drove peace away.
Nature herself gave utterance to her wrath,
And made the city tremble in her arms.
Affrighted conscience woke in many a breast,
And, as from Pilate's palace went of old
The hurried message, 'Have thou nought to do
With that just man,' so from Eudoxia flew
A letter full of pleas and penitence.

'Come back,' it said, 'thou holy man of God,
Whom wicked enemies have sorely wronged.'—
Hark to the signal! Yes, he comes! he comes!

[*The ship enters the harbor. Chrysostom is received with demonstrations of liveliest joy; and a torch-light procession escorts him to the church, where he is made to ascend the pulpit.*]

Chrys. What shall I say? Praise God forevermore!
I blessed Him when I went; I bless Him now.
The winter and the summer are not same,
But both unite to fertilize the field.
The Lord bade me withdraw and brought me back:
He sent the storm and sends the welcome calm.
For both alike I bless His holy name.
Praise God in prosperous times—they shall abide;
Praise God in adverse times—they shall depart.

LORD of the day and of the dark,
We glory in Thy gracious Name;
No wind-blown, evanescent spark,
It burns a pure and steadfast flame.

Thy name is LOVE, resplendent still
When prosperous suns expire or glow;
Its beams the sky of pleasure fill
And brightly tint grief's tearful bow.

The silver and the sable threads
　Together make life's fabric fair :
No perfect landscape but outspreads
　Some sober glooms amid the glare.

Oh LOVE most fond and firm and wise !
　Lead us the way Thou choosest well.
Where'er the changeful pathway lies
　A constant joy with us shall dwell.

VI.

PERSONS REPRESENTED.

CHRYSOSTOM, FLAVIAN, PAULUS, GLAUCUS,
OLYMPIAS, THEODORA.

SCENE.—*Constantinople and region of the Black Sea.*
TIME.—A. D. 404–407.

SCENE I.—*The Bishop's house in Constantinople.*

Enter CHRYSOSTOM *and* FLAVIAN.

Chrys. Again Herodias dances, and desires
The head of John.
Fla. I do not understand
What thou wouldst say.
Chrys. As if to cover up
The shame of short-lived penitence and fear,
Eudoxia dares with rites idolatrous
To challenge Heaven. Beside the church of God
She rears a silver statue of herself,
And bids the people bow and do it homage.
Fla. Thou wilt not think it duty to protest,
And on thy head bring down anew her wrath?
Chrys. What time the Babylonian King set up
A golden god in Dura, three brave men
Let not the seven-fold fires defeat their faith.
Shall we that live to-day be timorous
Before an irate woman, but provoke
With mad temerity the wrath of God?
My office were a nest of nettles if,
For dignity and safety, I should teach

My voice to utter aught but truth, or keep
A treacherous silence.. Nay, this haughty queen
Shall see her sin though fierce resentment fell
The hand that holds the mirror to her eyes.

Fla. Tis said that hired assassins wait and watch
To strike the dastard blow.

Chrys. And truly said.
The sanctity of home nor of God's house
Can lend protection to the man whose words
Are counted 'troublers unto Israel.'

Fla. Elijah fled the rage of Jezebel;
Wilt thou not, for our sake and that the cause
May yet receive thy service, fly the storm,
And in some foreign harbor furl the sails
That here so oft tempestuous winds have torn?

Chrys. One only harbor may afford me peace.
'The servant is not greater than his lord;'
The Christ through warfare entered into rest,
And we must suffer if we will be saved.
I will not imitate the prophet's flight,
But wait till violence shall thrust me forth.

Fla. The same decree that sends my bishop hence
Shall give me leave to share his banishment.

Chrys. Adversity reveals the faithful friend:
Yet shalt thou serve me best by serving those
I leave 'as sheep amidst the howling wolves.'

SCENE II.—*Room in the house of Olympias. Olympias reclining. A package of letters at her side.*

Olym. Companions of my weary solitude,
Ye tell me more than on your leaves is written.
I look upon you and the past comes back,
In living pictures dark and tragical.
I see again that night when sacrilege
Our holy house invaded, and the songs
Of Easter-time were turned to cries of fear,
And the baptismal font with blood was filled;
Not as when Pilate at the altar slew
For crime, but blood of youthful innocence.
I see the white-robed throng, who with the morn
Should march with music forth to celebrate
The risen Lord and their own life renewed,
By force expelled; and, as a leaf-crowned oak
Stripped bare of foliage by a thunderbolt,
The church at once bereft of worshippers.
I stand again with all the company
Of those who serve with Chrysostom, to hear
His words of farewell and of earnest charge:

Cheerful the tones, but heard by heavy hearts.
So sound the fallen chieftain's rallying words
To soldiers who in grief around him wait.
Again I watch upon the shore where fades
From sight the sail for far Bithynia bound.
Again fierce conflagration turns to dust
The house of God: and we that weep the loss
Are dragged to court, as the incendiaries.
The insolent Optatus, in the place
For judgment made, accuses me in terms
Of common slander, whose rebuke should burn
Within the breast and break from out the lips
That hate me most:—and he who would have helped
My weakness to sustain the blow, an exile.
Oh bitter months of persecution, pain
And grief! But ye have been my comforters,
Though oft renewing pain, epistles penned
In banishment.
Now let some fragrance steal
From out the store, to raise my fainting faith.
[*Takes up a letter and reads.*
'*The heavenly consolation comes to me*
As trouble calls. Who would have dreamed, my friend,
That in the storm, begirt with fog and night,
My little barque should navigate at ease

As if in quiet waters? So it is.
I only pray thy happiness may be
Not less than mine.'
Alas, a sterner storm
Drew nigh: the sentence came that banished him
To Cucusus, where torrid summers blaze,
And winters from the hills blow fiercely down,
And wild Isaurians devastate and kill.
Ah, then the wail that from our hearts arose
His own lament repeated. But anon
The wonted strain of *Praise to God* came back
To give us comfort, who in vain had sought
To tame the lioness who rules the state.

[*Takes a second letter.*

Oh this from Cæsarea brought a load
Of anguish; for it told the woful tale
Of toilsome journey o'er the rugged hills,
Beneath the blasting sun; of sickness, want,
And flight from savage men, where, in the dark,
Death laid his snares along the rocky slopes.
Yet gratitude toward God and human friends
Flows deep and strong through all the painful story.

[*Looks at other letters.*

And these from Cucusus.

[*Reads.*

'*Be not despondent;*

Nor exile nor imprisonment nor stripes
Are worthy to be called calamity,
But sin alone. Who injures not himself
Is safe. A little time, and all that mars
Our fair estate, shall pass away and leave
To immortality our wealth of joy.
From earthly help and earthly menacing
Look unto God, whose ways mysterious
Are ever merciful. To me, close-housed
In wintry Cucusus, He sends the gifts
That solace and relieve adversity.
Sabiniana and Dioscurus
Have made a home for me; and here my thoughts
Have leave to wander, though my feet are fast.
To far Phenicia, Persia, Antioch,
And you that suffer in the Capital
My frequent words convey my sympathy.
Nor can the distance, nor the frowning hills
And hostile hordes deter but some, inflamed
With youthful zeal, resort to me, as one
From whom they hope to learn the way of life.
What cause for thanks! although the best beloved
Are far away, and thronging cares do press
Their suit, sometimes, with importunity.'
Then came the short, impetuous summer heat,
Two dismal winters and the wild marauders.

And then disease and tedious days and nights
And the dispersion, when in clefts and caves,
As they in ancient times of whom the world
Was all unworthy, he was forced to hide
From the Isaurians, with multitudes
Who, closely pent, feared famine and infection.
Through snow and ice, by day and night, they
reach
The tower of Arabissus, scarce alive.
Alas, I know not if he lives to-day;
And life to me amidst such misery
Seems sometimes but a burden hard to bear.
God pity my infirmity! Again,
In silence, I will read this essay o'er
Whose lofty argument unfolds the law:
'*No harm for them that injure not themselves.*'

[*Enter* Attendant *and* PAULUS.

Your looks report no happy news for me.

Paul. Nay, lady; news that gives us all a pang:
The hounds that hunt the deer have found again
His hiding-place, and drive him forth to seek
New covert or to die.

Olym. And can no bribe
Nor argument at our command restrain
These fierce barbarians? are they so gross
In cruelty that they will rather kill

An innocent and helpless man than count
Whatever wealth we offer them his ransom?
Paul. Indeed, I would our dealings were with those
We call barbarians: some tenderness
Within their hearts might answer to our touch.
But fiercer, more relentless is the rage
That rules a woman's heart, when all the milk
Of natural gentleness has turned to gall,
Than is the violence of tribes untamed.
Eudoxia cannot sleep while burns the light
Of this pure life that shows her vanity
And sin. Not daring to extinguish it,
She would remove it where its power to draw
And to distress the gaze should cease: wherefore
She sends this order:
'*Let two soldiers lead*
The banished bishop forth to Pityus.'
Olym. Where lies the place?
Paul. Upon the empire's verge
Beneath Mount Caucasus, and on the shore
Where desolation looks along the sea.
To such a prison doth imperial wrath
Consign the prophet who would speak the truth.
Olym. Make haste to find what measures new may move

This purpose from its bent, or by what mode
Some succor may be sent ere 'tis too late.
Oh that my will could break the bonds that bind
This feeble body down! Then would I fly
To rescue him or perish at his side.

SCENE III.—*Church of St. Basiliscus in the province of Pontus.*

Enter two Soldiers.

First Sol. We ought to have heeded when he besought us to let him remain here till noon before attempting to proceed. Now we have had weary work to bring him back more dead than alive. To force him along was murder.

Second Sol. Have a care! If thou accusest me of murder I may feel obliged to save thee from the offence of lying, by matching deed to word.

First Sol. Be not angry; but I cannot see an inoffensive old man suffer without pity.

Second Sol. Pity is for women to feel. A Roman soldier ought to know nothing but to obey orders.

Besides, I like to give these holy people a little taste of hardship. We get kicks and curses enough from those in command: why not, when we have opportunity, pass some of them along to neighbors who are in danger of being spoiled by indulgence? If this woe-begone prisoner dies on our hands, why, we are saved the remainder of a most abominable journey. I'll go to sleep here in the corner; and you, if you choose, may devote your attentions to your charming patient.

First Sol. [*Goes to the chancel where Chrysostom lies, attended by Christian women of the neighborhood.*]

Forgive, oh holy man, my partnership
In cruelties I could not turn aside.

Chrys. I owe thee not forgiveness, but my thanks
For gentleness and kindest sympathy.
What thanks are due the Lord, that mine should be
A fate so like to His who heard harsh words
From one who hung beside Him, but the scorn
Rebuked and turned to reverence and prayer
By one who from the other cross beheld
His spirit entering into Paradise.

Woman. [*To her companions.*]

Prepare a litter; that, upon it laid,
He may be borne within some dwelling near.

Chrys. Content; the church of God hath been
my home;
Here will I die. Last night I saw the saint
Whose bones beneath this altar wait the day
Of resurrection. As my weary load
Of corporal pain fell off in sleep and left
The spirit buoyant and unveiled, behold,
A spirit glorified appeared and said:
'To-morrow thou shalt be with me in bliss.'
Kind friends, detain me not: but bring me here
The sacred symbols of my Saviour's death,
That once again with him assimilate
And crucified, I may be ready so
With him to rise and reign forevermore.
[*He takes the communion.*
Thank God for this! Thank God for everything!
[*Dies.*

First Sol. The words that oftenest left his living
lips
Seem lingering on them still. That settled smile
Hath in it *Praise to God.* Oh women, weep,
But not for him: weep for a world whose night
Hath lost its chiefest luminary.

Woman. Nay,
Within my heart a prophecy declares
The light, that sometime wandered midst the dark

And damp below, death's hand hath set on high,
A star whose beams shall shine undimmed by
years,
And draw the loving gaze of all the lands.

First Sol. With solemn ceremonies let us lay
The body to its rest beside the saint
Who long hath slumbered here. The time may be
When kings shall journey to this spot, and beg
The privilege to bear the dust away
Whose presence shall enrich the proudest shrine.

SCENE IV.—OLYMPIAS' *house. Present* OLYMPIAS, THEODORA, *and other deaconesses,* PAULUS, FLAVIAN, GLAUCUS, *and other ministers and friends.*

Glau. I loved him with you all, nor in my cell,
That shut from view the multitude of things
Within the earthly scene, was he forgotten
Who, on the earth, seemed yet a visitant
From heaven. I wrestled in my prayers for him.
But now he needs nor prayers nor sympathy
Save sympathy of joy ineffable.

Olym. But He who wept in grief beside the grave

Of Lazarus, will not rebuke our tears
For one so brave and good, from earth and us
Removed. Oh, might we but have been with him
When through death's valley dark alone he passed!

Fla. To me returns the ancient mystery,
How one who with such fervor served his God
Should fall beneath the scourge of sufferings
So keen and multiplied.

Paul. 'Whom God doth love
He chastens:' choicest gold doth tempt the art
Of the refiner and the graver most.
To prove the power of faith, the strong in faith
Must bear the weight of trials manifold,
That weak and unbelieving souls may see
And glorify celestial grace.

Theo. 'Whoso
Doth offer praise brings glory to our God.'
In darksome night, as well as cheerful day
The song of praise our heaven-taught warbler sang.

All. Lord, teach our souls to sing that harmony:
Forever make us to rejoice in Thee!

THE VALLEY OF BERACHAH.

(II. Chron. xx.)

WHEN Judah's foes were all assembled
Within Tekoa's wilderness,
On pallid lips the accents trembled:
'Save us, O Lord, in our distress!'

The answer came, their fears allaying,
'Ye shall not need to fight to-day;
For I Myself, My power displaying,
Will sweep that hostile host away.'

Forthwith, before the embattled legions,
A band of singers marched and sang;
And through those wild, infested regions
Praise to the Lord sublimely rang.

What frenzy then and dire delusion
That haughty, heathen host ran through!
Brothers and allies, in confusion,
With sword and spear each other slew.

Till lo, the watchman, far off gazing,
Beheld an army melt as snow:
And only spoils of wealth amazing
And fallen forms the field to show.

In earth's wide wilderness are thronging
The ranks of evil and of care:
And ofttimes, sad with fear and longing,
We pour our plaints in bitter prayer.

Oh could we sing our Lord's sweet praises
  Nor sin nor grief should do us harm;
But as, when morn her banner raises
  The wild beasts fly in strange alarm—

Our fears themselves should feel a panic;
  Perplexity should loose its toils,
And from the fallen host Satanic
  Our hands should gather happy spoils.

O Thou who art of grace the fountain,
  Help us in praise to find employ,
Till we ascend Thy heavenly mountain,
  With songs and everlasting joy!

NOTES.

Page 7.—'*See where her statue stands, a radiant queen*
Whose feet rest on the rising river-god,
Orontes.'

Allegorical Statue of Antioch.

[*From Conybeare and Howson's Life and Epistles of St. Paul.*

Page 7.—'*Mount Silphius, where the royal bird alighting*
Informed Seleucus here to found his city.'

According to tradition, the site of Antioch was determined by the flight of an eagle, with a piece of the flesh which Seleucus had offered in sacrifice.—[*See in Conybeare and Howson*, vol. i. p. 121.

Page 8.—' *the Vulcan crew*
That underneath this soil are wont to work.—'

The city, some of whose characteristic physical and social features are here pictured, has, during the last year, received an almost finishing blow from its old enemy, the earthquakes.

Page 9—' *The voice of Daphne calls her votaries.*'

Through an arcade paved with marble the path led toward Daphne, a pleasure grove five miles from the city.

"The establishment of a Greek Empire in Syria, on the death of Alexander the Great, involved the introduction of Grecian fable and mythology. Of all the fictions that poetry had rendered sacred and beautiful, there was none that experienced a readier or more enthusiastic reception in the East than that which had consecrated the fate of Daphne, and the story of Apollo's love. The god and the nymph were both adopted by the lively imaginations of their new votaries and

'that sweet grove
Of Daphne by Orontes,'

seemed fitter for the scene of such a tale than the cold clime of Greece. Here summer was tempered in its heat by hundreds of fountains; and an impenetrable laurel shade, that extended for miles, excluded the fiercer blaze of that sun whose worship imparted its sacred character to the place, and made it religious. The games which constituted so large a portion of the sacred rites in Greece were here performed with enthusiasm and devotion. Here, too, all who professed to worship were the votaries of love."—[*Lempriere's Dictionary.*—Art. *Daphne.*

Page 9.—'*Here's a Christian friend.*'

It will be borne in mind that as the name of Christianity became popular, many entered the church who were altogether wanting in the pure and self-denying spirit of the Master and his first disciples. The prevalent apostasy rendered such characters as that of Chrysostom the more noticeable and worthy of honor.

Page 10.—'*From Port Seleucia.*'

The port was at the mouth of the Orontes, while Antioch was a number of miles inland, but accessible by sail through the windings of the river.

Page 12.—'*The charioteer was dead.*'

The factious spirit and the sporting habit had wrought in Antioch, as elsewhere, a hardness and brutality of feeling under all the guise of gayety; and not seldom the festive games ended in hostile and sanguinary strife.

Page 15.—'*Anthusa.*'

The mother of Chrysostom is to be ranked with MONICA, the mother of Augustine, as an example of noble qualities and of what such qualities in a mother may effect for her children, and, through them, for the world.

Page 15.—'*Libanius.*'

This man was distinguished alike for his learning and teaching talent, and for his ardent championship of Paganism against Christianity. Anthusa seems to have judged—and rightly—that the faith she had inculcated on the mind of her son would only be rendered the more indelible by contact with an opposing faith.

Page 17.—'*The meek and matron robe was mine ere yet*
The years of youth were fled.'

The husband of Anthusa and father of Chrysostom was *Secundus*, an officer of high rank. At the time of his death, the son was just born and the mother only in her twentieth year.

Page 24.—'*They say he deals with dialectics less*
Than with the life.'

"The Christian orators who preceded him had been addicted to curious metaphysical disquisitions, and to fierce, ever-returning controversies with Pagans, Jews, and heretics, so called. Chrysostom was not wholly free from these defects; yet scarcely one of his predecessors so fully subordinated the subtlety of current dogmatic opinions to the interest of true piety and practical morality."—*Paniel.*

Page 25.—'*The rising waves of mutiny*—'

Antioch was under the immediate rule of a Governor, who was appointed by the Emperor at Constantinople. The present

Emperor, Theodosius the Great, had laid upon the city a tax disproportionate even to its abundant wealth. The dissatisfaction was general. It might not however have led to turbulence but for the action of a set of dissolute men who were habitually employed as *claqueurs* at the theatres, and who were ready for any riotous demonstration.

Page 41.—'*And when the proud Prime Minister returned*
From Antioch flushed with hope which he had bought
By bloodshed—'

Arcadius succeeded Theodosius, as Emperor of the East, in the year 395. As he was a weak character, the ambitious Prime Minister Rufinus aspired to be the 'power behind the throne' and more than the throne itself. To this end he planned a match between his daughter and the Emperor. But having appointed a certain Lucian to office in Antioch, he was chagrined to find that he had thereby incurred the displeasure of Arcadius. To remedy which error he hastened to Antioch and, upon some pretext, had Lucian arrested and put to death. But so atrocious an expedient signally failed—the beautiful ward of the murdered man being at that moment the accepted bride of the Emperor, through the cunning contrivance of the hairdresser, Eutropius.

Page 44.—'*—the proud Theophilus,*
Of Alexandria—'

Alexandria shared with Rome and Constantinople the honor of being a capital of the Roman Empire. Its patriarch, therefore, occupied a place of large power. Theophilus, the incumbent of the office at the present time, was a man of ability and energy, but of selfish schemes: wont to accommodate himself to circumstances, without overmuch regard for consistency or right principle; a natural enemy therefore of such a man as John Chrysostom.—[*Vide Neander's History of the Church.* vol. i pp. 689–692.

Page 45.—'*Olympias who serves the church so well.*'

The office of deaconess was instituted in the Apostolic age, and was of peculiar significance in Eastern countries, where the habits of society precluded men, in great degree, from ministering to families.—[*Ibid.* vol. i. p. 188.

Page 48.—'*The indolent resent our call to prayer*
That steals an hour from sleep.'

It was customary to have week-day services in the churches; but as most of the men made their business an excuse for non-attendance, Chrysostom instituted a nightly service of one hour. This, with the other requirements which his strict ideas dictated, came into sharp collision with the easy, careless and voluptuous style of things at the capital.

Page 53.—'*This traitor Tribigild with all his Goths.*'

The Gothic provinces were at this time tributary to the Empire. But their Generals, Tribigild and Gainas, living at the capital, became disgusted with the mercenary and oppressive administration of Eutropius, and determined upon revolt, if they could not otherwise secure his deposition.

Page 55.—' *Where fugitives, though tracked by justice, find Security.*'

Like the ancient "cities of refuge," the Christian churches were early recognized as inviolable asylums for all who fled to them for protection. It was this 'right of sanctuary' which Eutropius had caused to be repealed, because it stood in the way of his resentment.

Page 59.—' *The zeal that bade him brave the boisterous seas.*'

Not satisfied with the banishment of Eutropius, the Gothic Generals demanded the surrender into their hands of three other men who were in high office. With this demand the citizens were wholly unwilling to comply. But in a noble spirit of self-sacrifice the men voluntarily surrendered themselves, going into the midst of the hostile camp. Chrysostom lost no time in following them and pleading with the rough Generals for their safety.

Page 64.—' *An impulse such as sent Saint Christopher—*'

See the beautiful legend as told by Mrs. Jameson and the author of the 'Schönberg Cotta Family.'

Page 67.—' *When once they hear the church's censure seek Her altar nevermore, though penitent.*'

A sect, called Novatians, or Puritans, held that one who after baptism had received censure for gross sin, ought never to be re-admitted to church fellowship, however he might repent and hope for forgiveness with God.

Page 67.—‘ *The monks who in the Nitrian desert dwelt.*’

In the north of Egypt were two parties of monks. One party, residing in the *Nitrian* desert, accepted the doctrines of the celebrated Origen of Alexandria. The other party, in the *Scetic* desert, were strongly opposed to some of those doctrines. Theophilus, who had originally favored the Nitrian party, and had induced some of the leading men of that order to enter his service, found that they would not be subservient to his extravagant plans for spending the church revenues. Thereupon he put forth an edict forbidding any one to read the works of Origen. And when the monks would not obey, he instigated an armed attack, whereby the cloisters were destroyed and the poor monks, three hundred in number, were scattered. Eighty of them fled to the vicinity of Jerusalem; and on being driven thence embarked for Constantinople to seek shelter within the diocese of Chrysostom.—[*Perthes*, pp. 159, 160.

Page 71.—‘ *Within the dwelling of Eugraphia.*’

She was one of three court ladies whom the bishop had exasperated by the faithful severity of his criticism.

Page 84.—‘ *I see the white robed-throng who with the morn*
Should march with music forth—’

In the earlier ages of the Christian church, certain seasons were regarded specially appropriate for the observance of the ordinance of baptism; and of these seasons Easter eve was held to be the most sacred. Hence, in populous cities, multitudes, amounting sometimes to thousands, were baptized on this anniversary festival. The night time seems to have been chosen for the rite, in order to impart to it greater solemnity, perhaps mystery. On Easter morn the newly baptized appeared clad in white robes, emblematical of the new life of purity upon which they had entered.—[*Translators' note in Perthes*, p. 185.

Page 93.—' *When kings shall journey to this spot, and beg*
The privilege to bear the dust away—'

Arcadius died eight months after Chrysostom. Thirty years later, his son, Theodosius II. and the bishop Proclus brought the remains of Chrysostom, with the greatest honors, from Asia Minor to Constantinople. On the 27th of January, 438, Theodosius knelt down on his coffin and entreated forgiveness of the sainted spirit for the injustice which his parents, and especially his mother, had done him. Subsequently the bones of the now canonized hero were removed to Rome, and, about two centuries since, were deposited by Pope Urban VIII. in a chapel of St. Peter's which still bears the name of *Chrysostom*.—[*Ibid.* p, 231.

THE END.

www.ingramcontent.com/pod-product-compliance
Lightning Source LLC
LaVergne TN
LVHW021429110826
845150LV00007B/2157

* 9 7 8 1 4 2 5 5 0 7 1 1 4 *